Some Things Go Together

by **Charlotte Zolotow** • pictures by **Ashley Wolff**

HarperFestival®
A Division of HarperCollinsPublishers

Peace with dove
Home with love

Gardens with flowers
Clocks with hours

Moths with screen
Grass with green

Leaves with tree
and you with me

Mountains with high
Birds with fly

Witch with broom
Bowl with spoon

Pigeons with park
Stars with dark

Sand with sea
and you with me

Music with dance
Horses with prance

Hats with heads
Pillows with beds

Franks with beans
Kings with queens

Lions with zoo
and me with you

White with snow
Wind with blow

Moon with night
Sun with light